My ABC Storybook

Beat Eisele   **Catherine Yang Eisele**

Stephen M. Hanlon   **Rebecca York Hanlon**

Barbara Hojel

My ABC Storybook

Pearson Education, 10 Bank Street, White Plains, NY 10606

Vice president, director of publishing: Allen Ascher
Publisher: Anne Stribling
Senior development editor: Yoko Mia Hirano
Vice president, director of design and production: Rhea Banker
Executive managing editor: Linda Moser
Production manager: Alana Zdinak
Senior production editor: Mike Kemper
Senior manufacturing manager: Patrice Fraccio
Senior manufacturing buyer: Edie Pullman
Cover design: Rhea Banker and Lisa Donovan
Illustrator: Elaine Garvin
Art direction and production: Pearson Education Development Group

Library of Congress Cataloging-in-Publication Data

ISBN: 0-13-017587-0

2 3 4 5 6 7 8 9 10-WC-05 04 03 02

Contents

2

Aa

apple

ant

alligator

4

Bb

bus

backpack

book

6

Come on! Let's go!

Cc

cat

canoe

castle

Review

Aa

Bb

Cc

<u>a b c</u> d e f g h i j k l m n o p q r s t u v w x y z

Talk Time

Hi. I am Andy.

Becky

Carla

Don

Look! A deer!

Dd

doll

deer

duck

12

Ee

egg

elbow

elephant

13

15

Review

Dd

Ee

Ff

abc<u>def</u>ghijklmnopqrstuvwxyz

Talk Time

Is it a deer?

No.

Is it a duck?

Yes.

deer

elephant

fish

goose

goat

gate

19

Hh

horse

hat

house

21

22

Ii

instruments

inchworm

igloo

Gg

Hh

Ii

abcdef<u>ghi</u>jklmnopqrstuvwxyz

What color is it?

It's red.

blue

green

yellow

Jj

jam

jacket

jaguar

28

Kk

king

koala

key

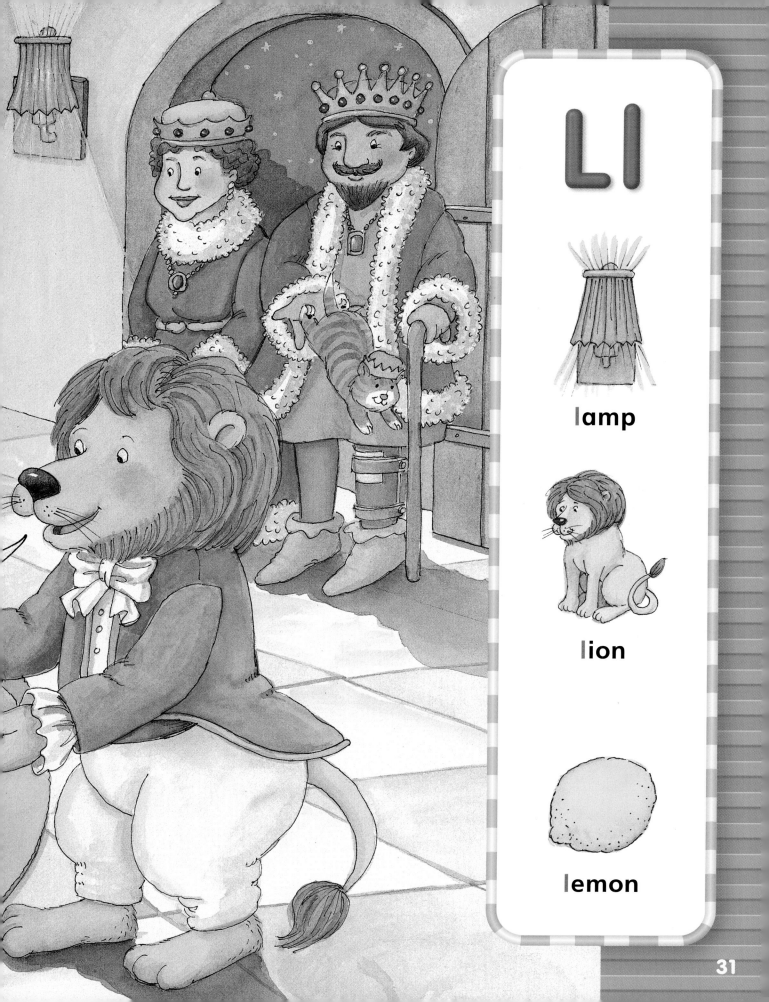

L l

lamp

lion

lemon

Review

Jj

Kk

Ll

Talk Time

Who's this?

This is my mother.

father

brother

sister

34

Mm

moon

monkey

map

38

O o

ox

octopus

ostrich

Review

Mm

Nn

Oo

Talk Time

It is my leg.

What is this?

nose

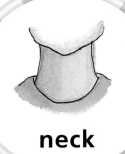

neck

mouth

No, I'm scared.

Qq

queen

quilt

quail

Review

Pp

Qq

Rr

abcdefghijklmno<u>pqr</u>stuvwxyz

50

Ss

sandwich

socks

snake

52

Tt

tiger

telephone

table

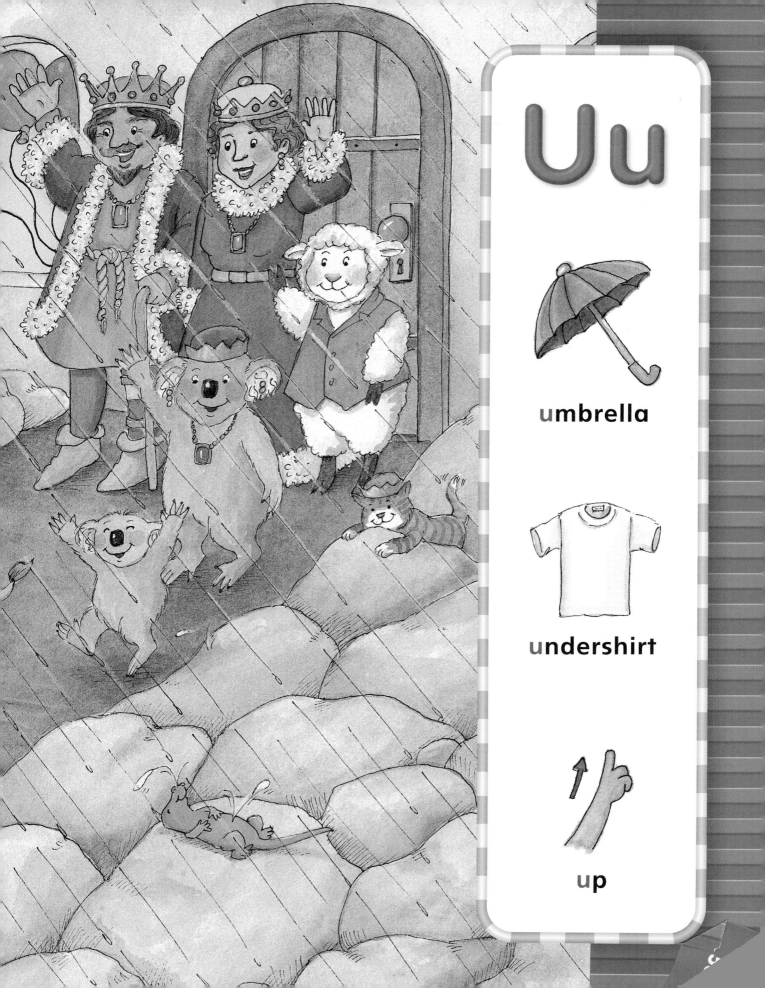

Uu

umbrella

undershirt

up

S s

T t

U u

abcdefghijklmnopqr<u>stu</u>vwxyz

Talk Time

Where is it?

It is in the box.

on

next to

under

I like vegetables.

Vv

van

vegetables

vet

60

Ww

web

water

watermelon

Xx

fo**x**

bo**x**

a**x**

Review

V v

W w

X x

7

8

9

10

Yy

yak

yawn

yo-yo

Review

Yy

Zz

abcdefghijklmnopqrstuvwx<u>yz</u>

70

Talk Time

I can speak English.

Yes, you can!

jump

walk

run

Alphabet
Adventure Photo Album

Point. Say.

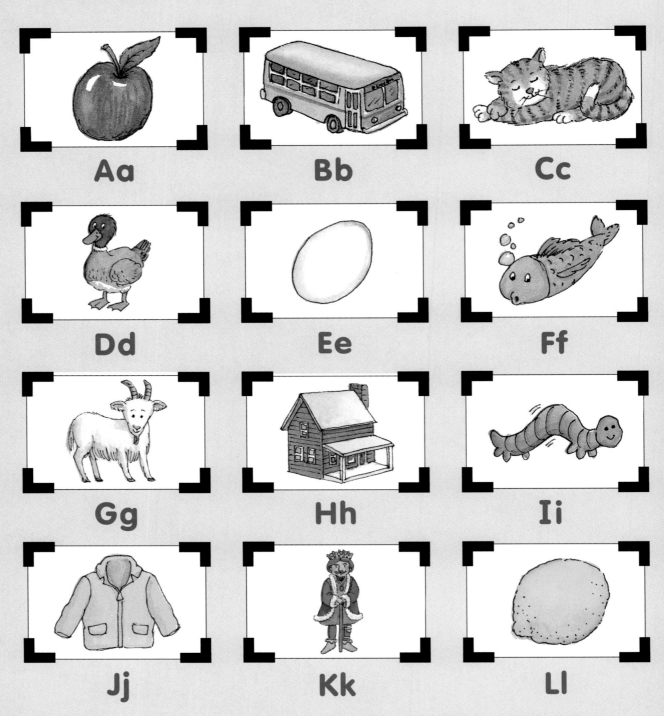

Aa

Bb

Cc

Dd

Ee

Ff

Gg

Hh

Ii

Jj

Kk

Ll

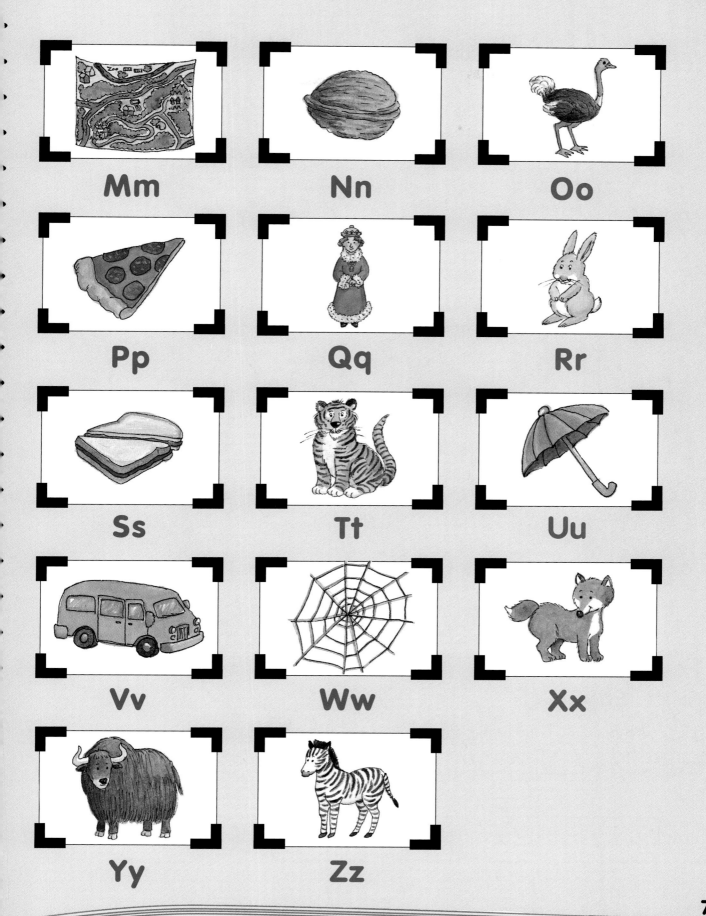

Mm

Nn

Oo

Pp

Qq

Rr

Ss

Tt

Uu

Vv

Ww

Xx

Yy

Zz

Shapes

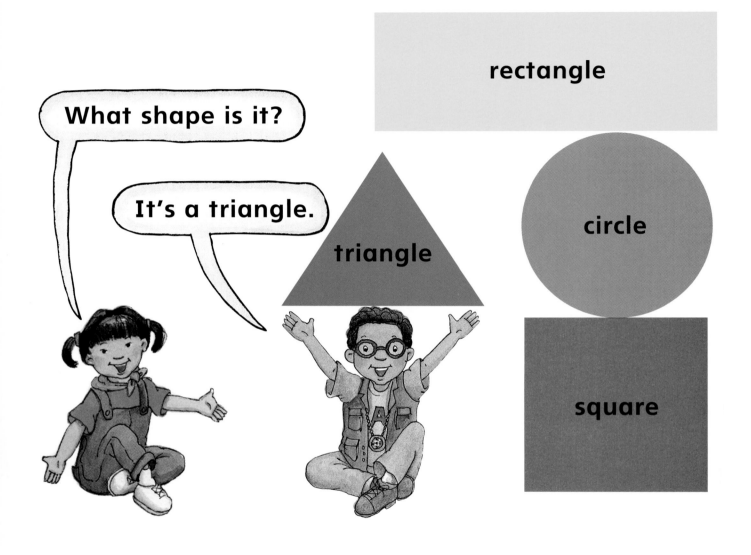

rectangle

What shape is it?

It's a triangle.

triangle

circle

square

Point. Say.

1.

2.

74

Days of the Week

What day is today?

It's Monday.

Monday	Tuesday	Wednesday	Thursday	Friday	Saturday	Sunday
1	2	3	4	5	6	7
8	9	10	11	12	13	14
15	16	17	18	19	20	21
22	23	24	25	26	27	28
29	30	31				

Scope and Sequence of My ABC Storybook

Unit	Letters	Story	Dialogue	Topics
1	Aa, Bb, Cc	One morning, Andy and Becky ride a bus to the river. They meet Carla and Don. Everyone gets into canoes to paddle down the river.	•Good morning, Andy. •Hi, Becky! Hello, Andy. •Hi, Carla and Don! Come on! Let's go! •Talk Time: Hi. I am ____.	Greetings Introductions Names
2	Dd, Ee, Ff	As the children paddle down the river, they see animals. They stop. Carla finds some big eggs. Don sees an elf on an elephant! They paddle away scared. Carla brings an egg.	•Look! A deer! •What is it? It's an egg. •I see a fish. •Talk Time: Is it a ____? Yes./No.	Animals Parts of the body Feelings Senses
3	Gg, Hh, Ii	The children see animals play a game. A cute monster, Figo, hatches from the egg! Becky's horn and a helicopter make lots of noise. Insects and instruments appear and Becky and Andy disappear down another part of the river.	•Wow! Look. Is it a girl? Is it a boy? •Help! Please stop! •What do you see? I see instruments! •Talk Time: What color is it? It's ____.	Animals Senses Instruments Colors
4	Jj, Kk, Ll	It gets windy. Carla and Don see a big castle and a jaguar. They stop and meet a king and sad Baby Koala at the castle. Baby Koala is looking for his mother. They go in the castle and Carla has lemonade.	•Do you see the castle? Yes, and I see a jaguar! •Hello, King. Hello, Koala. Where is my mother? •What's this? It's lemonade. •Talk Time: Who's this? This is my ____.	Weather Family members Animals Feelings
5	Mm, Nn, Oo	Baby Koala asks for help finding his mother. Don and Carla agree to help. They all go into the woods in the night darkness. Figo likes to eat Carla's nuts. They find a cave where they sleep and have strange dreams.	•Wait! Please help me. •It is night. I can't see. I can see. This way! •I like olives. •Talk Time: What is this? It is my ____.	Food Animals Parts of the Body Family Senses

Unit	Letters	Story	Dialogue	Topics
6	Pp, Qq, Rr	The next morning penguins walk by on the way to a party. One penguin leads them to Mama Koala stuck in a tree. The queen comes to help. When Mama Koala refuses to jump, Don ties a rope and Mama Koala climbs down. It begins raining and they go back to the castle.	•Penguin, where is my mama? I know. Follow me. •Please jump on the quilt. No, I'm scared. •It's raining! Let's go back. •Talk Time: How many? Let's count. ____.	Weather Food Feelings Animals Counting (1-5)
7	Ss, Tt, Uu	Carla and Don find their canoe at the river, and snakes scare them away. They return to the castle and everyone celebrates. The king and queen give Carla and Don a key to the castle. Then the children and Figo say good-bye and ride a tiger to a van to go home.	•What are they? They are snakes! •Take this home. Thank you. •Good-bye! Good-bye! Thanks for the umbrella. •Talk Time: Where is it? It is ____ the box.	Clothing Food Manners Prepositions Animals
8	Vv, Ww, Xx	The children find a vegetable garden by the van. A goose plays a violin. A vet takes them home in his van. On the way, they stop at a waterfall because Don is thirsty. The vet takes a fox with chicken pox to the zoo.	•I like vegetables. •I'm thirsty. I see water. Please stop! •What's that? The fox has chicken pox. •Talk Time: How old are you? I'm ____.	Food Senses Animals Ages Counting (6-10)
9	Yy, Zz	Carla and Don get out of the van at Andy's house. Andy and Becky are waiting for them. Everybody is happy, but Figo is missing! The children look around the zoo and finally find Figo eating nuts under a tree.	•I'm so happy to see you! •It's Figo! I love the zoo. •Talk Time: I can ____. Yes, you can!	Feelings Animals Verbs
Concepts			•What shape is it? It's a ____. •What day is today? It's ____.	Alphabet Shapes Days of the Week Food

Word List

abcdefghijklmnopqrstuvwxyz